The Cool, Awesome, Simple Science Series

Hands-On Chemistry

for Elementary Grades

by

Phil Parratore

Table of Contents

Acid/Base
Fizzies

What You Will Do

Verify the existence of carbonation.

Get it Together

- 1 Tbsp. baking soda
- 6 Tbsp. powdered sugar
- 1 envelope unsweetened powdered soft drink mix
- Small bowl
- Glass of chilled water
- Tablespoon

Procedure

1. Mix all powdered ingredients together in a bowl.
2. Stir one heaping tablespoon of the mixture into the water. Stir and observe.
3. Taste the solution.

A Closer Look

You have made a drinkable acid/base reaction. The powdered soft drink mix contains citric acid which reacts with the baking soda, a base. When the molecules come together, there is a chemical reaction that produces fizzy bubbles of carbon dioxide gas.

Clean Up

Store the powder in a container.

3

Hair Today, Not Tomorrow

5 minutes+

What You Will Do

Display how bleach dissolves human hair.

Get it Together

- ◆ Clump of human hair (about the length of a walnut)
- ◆ Chlorine bleach
- ◆ Small jar
- ◆ Spoon

Procedure

1. Collect a small sample of hair from a local barber or beauty salon.
2. Fill the jar about half full of bleach.
3. Place the hair in the bleach. Use the spoon to push the hair into the bleach.
4. Allow the jar to sit undisturbed for about 30 minutes.

A Closer Look

The hair starts to dissolve. Bleach is a basic chemical while hair is acidic. The combination of an acid and a base is called a neutralization reaction. Bleach can dissolve any fiber that is an acid. Bleach is safe to use on cotton because cotton is also basic, but it will dissolve wool, which is weakly acidic.

Attention!

Use caution when working with bleach. Do not get on your skin or clothing.

I'm in a Jam

10 minutes

What You Will Do

Show how fruit can be used to detect acids and bases.

Get it Together

- Strawberry jam or jelly
- Eye dropper
- Ammonia
- Glass of warm water
- Vinegar
- Tablespoon

Procedure

1. Place a tablespoon of the jam in a glass of warm water. Observe the color.
2. Place a few drops of ammonia in the same glass. Stir and observe the color.
3. Add a few drops of vinegar. Stir and observe the color.

A Closer Look

Jam is a natural indicator that tells whether a substance is an acid or a base by changing colors. When you added a few drops of ammonia to the jam/water mixture, it turned a greenish-purple, indicating the presence of a base. When you added vinegar, an acid, it turned red.

Attention!
Use caution when working with ammonia.

Clean Up

Flush all the used material down the drain.

5

My Pop is Tops

5 minutes

What You Will Do

Make a carbonated soft drink.

Get it Together

- ½ tsp. vanilla extract
- Cinnamon
- ½ glass of water
- 3 Tbsp. sugar
- ½ tsp. lemon or lime juice
- 1 tsp. baking soda
- Drinking glass

A Closer Look

The baking soda (a chemical base) mixes with the acid from the lemon/lime juice to produce carbon dioxide gas. This process is called carbonization.

Procedure

1. Fill the glass about half full of water.
2. Add the sugar, vanilla extract, cinnamon, and lemon or lime juice to the water. Stir.
3. Add the baking soda. Stir.

Clean Up

Drink it up. Add ice if desired.

What Now?

Try making other flavors using orange or grape juice.

Acid/Base
We Eat Acids and Bases?

20 minutes

What You Will Do

Demonstrate a neutralization reaction.

Get it Together

- Red cabbage
- Pot
- Water
- Stove

- Lemon juice
- Ammonia
- 3 clear cups
- 3 eye droppers

Procedure

1. Make cabbage juice by placing red cabbage leaves in a pot of boiling water for about 15 minutes until the water is deep red.
2. Discard the leaves.
3. Place five drops of the juice into three separate cups.
4. Using a second eye dropper, add 10 drops of lemon juice (an acid) to one cup.
5. Using a third eye dropper, add 10 drops of ammonia (base) to the second cup.
6. Keep the third cup for comparison.
7. Now add ammonia, one drop at a time, to the cup containing lemon juice. Keep adding ammonia until the color no longer changes.
8. Add lemon juice, one drop at a time, to the ammonia until the color no longer changes.

A Closer Look

A neutralization reaction is a reaction between an acid and a base. Cabbage juice turns red in the presence of an acid (lemon juice) because the acid changes the cabbage molecules. When a base (ammonia) is added to the cabbage/acid mixture, the cabbage molecules, first return to their original state, or they are neutralized. As more base is added, the cabbage molecules change again, this time turning green. The opposite occurs when you add lemon juice to your cabbage/base mixture. Cabbage juice is another natural indicator which can tell the difference between an acid and a base.

Attention!

Do not mix up your eye droppers.

What Now?

Try using your cabbage juice indicator on other common kitchen items.

7

Chemical Change
A Sticky Situation

15 minutes+

What You Will Do

Illustrate how glue can be extracted from milk.

Get it Together

- ¼ cup skim milk
- Filter paper or coffee filter
- Paper cup
- 1 Tbsp. vinegar
- Pinch of baking soda
- Funnel
- Ice cream stick
- 2 small jars or cups

Procedure

1. Place the vinegar and skim milk into a jar. Stir with the ice cream stick.
2. Place the filter paper in the funnel and set it into the second jar.
3. Pour the vinegar/milk solution through the filter into the second jar. It will take about ten minutes to drip through.
4. Carefully scrape the white curds remaining in the filter paper and place them into the paper cup.
5. Discard the liquid (whey) in the second jar.
6. Add a pinch of baking soda to the curds. Stir.
7. If the glue is too thick, add a small amount of water.
8. Glue some paper together and allow it to dry overnight.

A Closer Look

Milk contains a protein called casein. It can be extracted from milk by adding an acid (vinegar). The acid causes the casein to clump together. When it is neutralized (with baking soda) the casein can be made into a white glue that dries clear. In our procedure, the curds are separated from the whey. The curds remain in the filter and are used for making the glue. The whey, which is mostly water and sugar, passes through the filter paper. This process is similar to the making of cottage cheese.

Chemical Change
Alka-Pop

2 minutes

What You Will Do

Display how a gas forms in a chemical reaction.

Get it Together

◆ 35-mm plastic film canister with a snap lid
◆ Effervescent antacid tablet
◆ Eye dropper
◆ Water

Procedure

1. Break the antacid tablet into three equal portions.
2. Place one of the broken pieces into the film canister.
3. Fill the eyedropper with water and place 20 drops of water in the canister.
4. Snap the lid on firmly and swirl once to mix the tablet and water.
5. Place the canister on a flat surface, away from people and objects.
6. Stand back and observe.

A Closer Look

The antacid is very reactive in water. The pressure of the released carbon dioxide gas builds up inside the film canister until the lid pops off. This is a good example of what happens when gases are under pressure.

Attention!

After placing the top on the film canister, do not stand over it. Do only under adult supervision.

Clean Up

Wash and dry the canister before repeating the experiment again.

What Now?

Try to dissolve the tablets in different types of liquids such as vinegar and lemon juice. Time the reaction.

Chemical Change
Baby Got Gas!

3 minutes

What You Will Do

Illustrate the amount of carbon dioxide gas dissolved in carbonated beverages.

Get it Together

- Baby bottle with nipple
- Open can of cold carbonated soda

Procedure

1. Pour the soda into the bottle and put the top on.
2. Pinch the nipple of the bottle closed and shake it for 30 seconds.
3. Hold the bottle downward and release the nipple.

A Closer Look

Shaking the bottle causes the carbon dioxide gas particles in the carbonated beverage to move faster by increasing the pressure inside the bottle. Carbon dioxide is a soluble gas that dissolves in all carbonated beverages.

Attention!

Do not point the bottle at anyone. If possible, do this experiment outdoors because it is messy.

What Now?

Repeat this experiment with a warm can of soda.

10

Curds and Whey

3 minutes

What You Will Do

Separate milk into its solid and liquid parts.

Get it Together

◆ Small jar with lid
◆ Fresh milk
◆ 2 Tbsp. vinegar
◆ Tablespoon

Procedure

1. Fill the jar ³/₄ full of milk.
2. Add two tablespoons of vinegar.
3. Allow the jar to sit for a few minutes.

A Closer Look

The solid particles in the milk are evenly spread throughout the liquid. The vinegar, which is a weak acid, causes the solid particles to clump together and form the solid curd. The liquid that remains is the whey. A mixture of liquids with solid particles spread throughout is called a colloid. Milk is an example of a colloid.

Chemical Change
Don't "Steel" from Me

5 minutes+

What You Will Do

Observe different characteristics of metal alloys.

Get it Together

- ◆ 2 different types of nails
- ◆ 2 different sizes of stainless steel bolts
- ◆ Sealable plastic bag
- ◆ 1 cup saltwater
- ◆ Paper towel

Procedure

1. Wrap the nails and bolts in the paper towel.
2. Place the towel in the plastic bag.
3. Add the salt water and seal the bag.
4. Check on the metals after one day, then after two days.

A Closer Look

The nails rusted while the bolts did not rust or rusted very little. Both materials are made from metal alloys. An alloy is a substance made of two or more elements and has properties of metal. The carbon-based steel in the nail, similar to the hull of a ship, rusted the most because of a chemical reaction with the salt and the water. The stainless steel bolt is made from a different rust-resistant alloy.

Attention!
Avoid getting salt in your eyes.

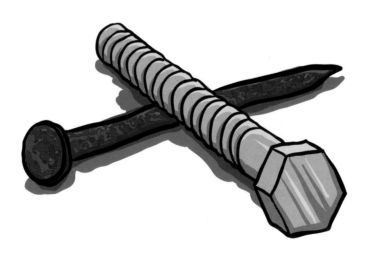

Clean Up

Put the nails and bag in the trash. Rinse the salt water down the sink.

12

Chemical Change
Eggs-periment

2 minutes+

What You Will Do

Examine how fluoride protects the enamel on teeth from being eaten away by acids.

Get it Together

- ◆ 2 hard-boiled eggs
- ◆ Jar with lid
- ◆ Vinegar
- ◆ Fluoride mouthwash

Procedure

1. Place one egg in the jar with the fluoride mouthwash. Make sure the mouthwash completely covers the egg.
2. Cap the jar and allow it to sit for 24 hours.
3. Remove the fluoride egg from the jar, flush the liquid down the drain, and rinse the jar with clean water.
4. Place both eggs in the clean jar.
5. Fill the jar with vinegar. Make sure the vinegar completely covers both eggs.
6. Cap the jar and allow it to sit for 24 hours.
7. Remove both eggs from the jar and carefully squeeze both of them.

A Closer Look

The shell of the egg soaked in fluoride will be harder than the egg not soaked in the rinse. The vinegar, a weak acid, eats through the non-treated egg, while the fluoride forms a protective layer over the treated egg. Tooth enamel can be compared to the shell of an egg because both are hard, protective outer layers. Vinegar acts like certain mouth acids that promote tooth decay. Using a fluoride mouthwash daily can combat these mouth acids and keep your teeth strong.

13

Chemical Change
Electric Lemon

10 minutes

What You Will Do

Use lemon juice to make a battery.

Get it Together

- ◆ Whole lemon
- ◆ Clean nail
- ◆ Several inches of non-insulated copper wire
- ◆ Headphones

Procedure

1. Stick the nail and one end of the copper wire in the lemon.
2. Bend the wire so the free end comes close to the nail, but does not touch it.
3. Place the headphones on your head.
4. Touch the headphone plug to the nail and the wire at the same time until you hear a static sound.

A Closer Look

The lemon juice in this experiment acts as an electrolyte, a liquid that conducts electricity. When you add a negative electrode (nail) and a positive electrode (copper wire), you have created a battery. When the headphones made contact with the metals, an electric current flowed through them causing the static sound. The sound is created when contact is made and once again when contact is broken.

What Now?

Slide the headphone plug along the wire and the nail.

Chemical Change
Firefighter

4 minutes

What You Will Do

Show how carbon dioxide puts out fires.

Get it Together

◆ Quart (or smaller) jar with screw lid
◆ Baking soda
◆ Vinegar
◆ Matches
◆ Tablespoon

Procedure

1. Place 3 to 4 tablespoons of baking soda in the jar.
2. Quickly pour about 3 to 4 tablespoons of vinegar in the jar.
3. Screw the lid on the jar.
4. After the mixture stops bubbling, light the match.
5. Open the jar and hold the lit match over the mouth of the jar.

A Closer Look

The match quickly went out because the chemical reaction of the baking soda and the vinegar produced carbon dioxide. The oxygen in the jar was used up during the reaction to make the carbon dioxide. Carbon dioxide gas and foam are commonly used in fire extinguishers.

Attention!
Use caution when working with matches. Do only under adult supervision.

Chemical Change
Floating Pasta

2 minutes

What You Will Do

Demonstrate how a chemical reaction can move objects.

Get it Together

- Uncooked pasta
- Glass container
- Vinegar
- Baking soda
- Tablespoon
- Water

Procedure

1. Place two cups of water in the container.
2. Dissolve one tablespoon of baking soda in the water.
3. Place the pasta in the container.
4. Now stir in four tablespoons of vinegar and observe.

What Now?

If the reaction starts to slow down, add more vinegar.

Chemical Change
I Got Nailed

25 minutes

What You Will Do

Demonstrate the process of electroplating.

Get it Together

- ◆ 4 ounces of lemon juice or vinegar
- ◆ 6 dull copper coins
- ◆ Large, clean nail
- ◆ Pinch of salt
- ◆ Small jar
- ◆ Sandpaper

A Closer Look

Copper from the coins interacted with the acid from the lemon juice and coated the nail. This new chemical is called copper citrate. When you inserted the nail into the solution, the nail got electroplated with a thin layer of copper that cannot be rubbed off.

Procedure

1. Place the coins in the jar and cover them with lemon juice.
2. Add the salt and stir.
3. Allow to stand for 5 minutes.
4. Clean the nail with the sandpaper.
5. Place the nail in the solution.
6. Allow to stand for 15 minutes.
7. Remove the nail.

Clean Up

Rinse the coins and flush the liquid down the drain.

Irish Soda Bread

15 minutes+

What You Will Do

Show that baking causes a chemical reaction.

Get it Together

- 3 cups whole-wheat flour
- 1 cup all-purpose flour
- 1 Tbsp. salt
- 1 tsp. baking soda
- $^3/_4$ tsp. double-acting baking powder
- 1$^2/_3$ cups buttermilk
- Mixing bowl
- Buttered 8" cake pan
- Oven

A Closer Look

Baking involves chemical reactions when baking soda and baking powder are used. Following the reaction, you get an entirely new substance, in this case, Irish soda bread.

Attention!

Follow the directions carefully and make sure you wash your hands before you begin.

Procedure

1. Combine the dry ingredients and mix thoroughly.
2. Add the buttermilk to make a soft dough.
3. Knead on a lightly floured board for 2 or 3 minutes.
4. Form into a round loaf and place in the cake pan.
5. Bake in a preheated oven at 375°F for 35-40 minutes.
6. Let the loaf cool before cutting and enjoying.

Chemical Change
Is My Apple Ripe?

5 minutes

What You Will Do

Show the presence of starch in fruit.

Get it Together

◆ An apple
◆ Tincture of iodine solution (drug store)
◆ Knife

Procedure

1. Cut the apple in half.
2. Pour a small amount of iodine on the cut surface, draining away any excess.
3. Allow the apple to stand for a few minutes.

A Closer Look

As apples ripen, the starch in the fruit turns into sugar. To see if an apple is ripe, harvesters test the fruit for the presence of starch using iodine. Starch reacts with iodine to give a blue-black color while sugar does not. If your apple has no blue-black color, it is ripe. If there is some stain, it is not completely ripe, and if there is a lot of stain, and therefore, a lot of starch, it is not ready to eat.

Attention!
Iodine stains and is poisonous. Use only under adult supervision.

What Now?

Try this test on other fruit.

Chemical Change
Pop Do Wop!

1 minute

What You Will Do

Observe effervescence.

Get it Together

- ◆ Clear glass
- ◆ Carbonated soda
- ◆ 1 tsp. table salt

Procedure

1. Fill the glass ½ way with the soda.
2. Add the salt to the soda.

A Closer Look

In this demonstration, the salt reacted with the soda and caused excess carbon dioxide gas to be released. Effervescence means to give off bubbles of gas.

Clean Up

Have some paper towels ready as the reaction may overflow.

Chemical Change
Punch Out

2 minutes

What You Will Do

Demonstrate the power of bleach.

Get it Together

- 2 clear glasses, the same size
- Water
- 2 Tbsp. bleach
- Red food coloring
- Measuring spoon

A Closer Look

The liquid turns clear. Laundry bleach contains a chemical called sodium chlorate. This chemical contains oxygen which is easily released. It combines with chemicals in food coloring to make a colorless compound.

Procedure

1. Fill one glass with ¾ cups of water and add three drops of food coloring.
2. Place the bleach in the second glass.
3. Pour the colored water into the glass with the bleach. Stir.

Attention!

Do only under adult supervision. Use caution when working with bleach. Use proper ventilation with bleach.

Clean Up

Flush the liquids down the drain.

21

Chemical Change
Sink Your Teeth into This

3 minutes

What You Will Do

Demonstrate an unusual way to brush your teeth.

Get it Together

- Toothbrush
- Fresh bottle of club soda or ginger ale
- Toothpaste
- Water

Procedure

1. Brush half your teeth with toothpaste. Rinse with water.
2. Brush the remainder of your teeth with toothpaste.
3. Rinse with the club soda or ginger ale instead of water.
4. Spit, and spit, and spit.

A Closer Look

Club soda and gingerale contain carbon dioxide. When it sloshed around in your mouth, and mixed with saliva and toothpaste, these other ingredients pushed the carbon dioxide out, forming many, many bubbles. This, along with the glycerin in the toothpaste, keeps you foaming at the mouth.

Attention!
Do not swallow the mixture.

22

Chemical Change
This Reaction is Cool

2 minutes

What You Will Do

Demonstrate an endothermic chemical reaction.

Get it Together

◆ 3 Tbsp. baking soda
◆ ½ cup vinegar
◆ Plastic cup

Procedure

1. Place the baking soda in the cup.
2. Pour in the vinegar.
3. Feel the outside of the cup for a moment.

A Closer Look

The chemical reaction of baking soda and vinegar produces carbon dioxide gas. As with any chemical reaction, there is a temperature change. In this case, heat energy is being absorbed by the reaction, making the glass feel cooler. We call this type of reaction endothermic. The opposite of an endothermic reaction is an exothermic reaction—when heat energy is given off and heat is produced.

Attention!
Hold this over a sink because it might overflow.

23

Chemical Change
What a Lemon

30 minutes

What You Will Do

Demonstrate the chemical breakdown of lemon juice.

Get it Together

- Fresh lemon
- Cotton swab
- Desk lamp
- Paper
- Water
- Cup

Procedure

1. Squeeze all the juice from the lemon into the cup.
2. Add an ounce or two of water. Stir.
3. Use the swab and write a secret message on the paper.
4. Wait for the message to dry.
5. Turn on the desk lamp and hold the paper over the bulb for a few minutes.
6. Read your secret message.

A Closer Look

At first the message is hard to see because of the light color of the lemon juice. When the heat from the lamp evaporated the water, the oxygen in the air reacted with the remaining citric acid, causing it to turn brown.

Attention!

Be careful not to burn yourself with the heat from the desk lamp.

24

Chemical Change
Yeast Creature

20 minutes

What You Will Do

Show how yeast is a living organism.

Get it Together

- Dried yeast
- 1 tsp. sugar
- Balloon
- Glass bottle
- Warm water
- Bowl

Procedure

1. Mix the package of yeast with two tablespoons of warm water in the bottle.
2. Stir in the sugar.
3. Stretch the balloon over the neck of the bottle.
4. Stand the bottle in a bowl of water for about 15 minutes.

© Carson-Dellosa CD-7323

A Bowl of Bubbles

10 minutes

What You Will Do

Illustrate sublimation.

Get it Together

- Chunk of dry ice
- Clear bowl or large glass
- Soap and bubble wand

Procedure

1. Place the dry ice in the bowl and allow it to completely evaporate.
2. Blow a few soap bubbles and allow them to settle in the bottom of the bowl.

A Closer Look

The bubbles seem to float in the bowl. Dry ice is frozen carbon dioxide. Instead of melting to a liquid, it changes directly from a solid to a gas. This is called sublimation. The dry ice sublimed in the bowl and formed a denser layer of carbon dioxide gas at the bottom of the bowl. When the soap bubbles landed on the layer of carbon dioxide gas, it seemed to form an invisible cushion. The carbon dioxide gas sits in the bottom of the bowl because it is more dense than the air around it.

Attention!

Do not touch the dry ice with your hand—it will cause severe burns. Do this activity only under adult supervision.

Clean Up

Flush the dry ice down the drain with water.

Density
Sphere of Oil

3 minutes

What You Will Do

Compare the densities of alcohol, water, and oil.

Get it Together

- ◆ Clean drinking glass
- ◆ ½ cup rubbing alcohol
- ◆ ½ cup water
- ◆ Cooking oil
- ◆ Eyedropper

Procedure

1. Pour the water in the glass.
2. Tilt the glass and very slowly pour in the alcohol. Be careful not to shake the glass as you do not want to mix the two liquids.
3. Fill the eyedropper with oil.
4. Place the tip of the eyedropper below the surface of the top alcohol layer and squeeze out several drops of oil.

A Closer Look

The alcohol is less dense than the water and floats on top of it. The oil is more dense than the alcohol, but less dense than the water so it sinks below the alcohol level, but not below the water level. The oil molecules are strongly attracted to each other and strongly repelled by alcohol and water. The attractive forces of the oil are equal on all sides, resulting in the formation of a perfect sphere.

27

Wave Bye-Bye

2 minutes

What You Will Do

Demonstrate a hand-held wave machine.

Get it Together

- Quart-size resealable bag
- Blue food coloring
- Bottle of mineral oil
- Water

A Closer Look

The mineral oil is less dense than the water and, therefore, will "float" on the surface. The more dense material will always "sink" to the bottom.

Procedure

1. Fill the bag half full of water.
2. Add a few drops of food coloring.
3. Fill the rest of the bag with mineral oil.
4. Get as much air out of the bag as possible, then seal it.
5. Rock the bag back and forth.

Clean Up

Place the sealed bag and its contents in the trash.

What Now?

Try the mixture with different liquids. Add solids and see where they end up in relation to the liquids.

28

Flammability

A Burning Question

1 minute

What You Will Do

Show that carbon dioxide gas will not support a flame.

Get it Together

- ◆ Freshly opened carbonated beverage
- ◆ Glass
- ◆ Matches

Procedure

1. Pour the carbonated beverage into the glass.
2. Carefully light the match and place it over the glass.

A Closer Look

The match is quickly extinguished when you hold it over the beverage. This is because flames need oxygen in order to burn. The carbon dioxide from the beverage is under a fair amount of pressure and when the bubbles burst at the surface, oxygen is pushed out of the way. The carbon dioxide starves the flame of oxygen, and that is why the flame quickly goes out. Carbon dioxide is used in many kinds of fire extinguishers.

Attention!
Use caution when working with matches. Do only under adult supervision.

29

Let's Have a Blast

5 minutes

What You Will Do

Show how a combustion engine works in an automobile.

Get it Together

- Clean, 1-gallon plastic milk or water container with lid
- 5 Tbsp. rubbing alcohol
- Long lighter
- Dark room
- Table

Procedure

1. Pour the alcohol into a clean container.
2. Put the lid on and shake the container for about 30 seconds.
3. Hold the container upright and remove the lid for a few seconds.
4. Replace the lid and shake for another 30 seconds.
5. Remove the lid and pour the alcohol back into the alcohol bottle.
6. Place the container in the center of a sturdy table.
7. Have everyone stand back while an adult removes the lid.
8. An adult should ignite the lighter and place the flame over the mouth of the container.

A Closer Look

You see a bluish flame shoot out and you hear a "swoosh." You have vaporized the alcohol, or, turned it from a liquid to a gas. The flame ingnites the vapors, causing an explosion. In an automobile's engine, the heat and pressure from a controlled explosion of gasoline act directly on the moving parts of an engine giving it power to move the vehicle.

Attention!

Do only under adult supervision. An adult should light the vapors at arm's length.

What Now?

Try to repeat this experiment. Nothing will happen until you completely fill the container with water and rinse it out. Rinsing out the container removes carbon dioxide gas and puts in a fresh supply of oxygen.

Flammability

Lemon Fireworks

3 minutes

What You Will Do

Display the flammability of lemon oil.

Get it Together

- Whole lemon
- Candle
- Match
- Knife

Procedure

1. Cut a large chunk of peel from the lemon.
2. Light the candle.
3. Squeeze the lemon peel near the flame. Observe.

A Closer Look

As the lemon peel is bent, some of its oil and water squirt into the flame. The oil burns as it passes through the flame while the water evaporates. This causes a sparkle, or fireworks.

Attention!

Use caution when working with a flame. Do only under adult supervision.

31

Flammability

Money to Burn

5 minutes

What You Will Do

Display the difference between water and rubbing alcohol in the presence of heat.

Get it Together

- ◆ Container of $^{50}/_{50}$ water/rubbing alcohol solution
- ◆ Dollar bill
- ◆ Pliers
- ◆ Lighter
- ◆ Paper towel
- ◆ Dark room

A Closer Look

Alcohol ignites quickly in the presence of fire while water can absorb a great deal of heat. Your dollar bill did not burn because it was protected from the flames by a layer of water.

Procedure

1. Dip the dollar bill in the water/rubbing alcohol mixture for about 10 seconds. Make sure it is fully submerged.
2. Hold the bill with the pliers over a paper towel away from the mixture.
3. Turn off the light.
4. Light the bill from the bottom.

Attention!

Do only under adult supervision. Keep sleeves, hair and fingers away from open flames.

32

Flammability

What a Gas!

10 minutes

What You Will Do

Display how fire can be extinguished by carbon dioxide gas.

Get it Together

- ◆ Pie pan
- ◆ Small candle
- ◆ Clay or candle holder
- ◆ Drinking glass
- ◆ ¼ cup vinegar
- ◆ ¼ cup water
- ◆ 1 Tbsp. baking soda
- ◆ Spoon
- ◆ Matches

A Closer Look

Carbon dioxide gas was produced by the chemical reaction of the baking soda and the vinegar. Carbon dioxide is a colorless gas that extinguished the flame.

Attention!
Use caution when working with matches.

Procedure

1. Secure the candle in a holder or some clay and place it in the center of the pie pan.
2. Place the baking soda in the glass and add the water.
3. Light the candle.
4. Add the vinegar and stir with the spoon.
5. As soon as the mixture stops foaming, tip the glass as if you were pouring something out of it onto the flame. Do not pour any liquid on the candle.
6. Observe what happens to the flame.

What Now?

Try other powders, such as flour or sugar and see if you get the same results.

Flammability

You're Nuts!

1 minute

What You Will Do

Prove that the food we eat contains energy.

Get it Together

- Dry roasted nut
- Match or lighter
- Long tweezers

Procedure

1. Hold the nut with the tweezers.
2. Carefully place a lit match or lighter under the nut until it starts to burn.
3. Remove the lighter.

A Closer Look

Three things are needed for something to burn—fuel, a heat source, and oxygen in the air. The oil in the nut is almost 100% fat, which is the fuel. Fat burns and produces energy. The nut will stay on fire until all the fat is burned off. Once the fuel is gone you are left with black, charred carbon. All living things contain carbon.

Attention!

Do this only under adult supervision. Use caution when working with fire.

Heat Energy
Do You Have a Long Fuse?

5 minutes

What You Will Do

Illustrate how a fuse works.

Get it Together

- Two 6" pieces of insulated wire with exposed metal tips
- 9-volt battery
- Cartridge fuse, 1 ampere maximum (hardware store)
- Tape

Procedure

1. Observe the fuse and notice the small piece of metal that runs through it.
2. Tape one end of each piece of wire to the battery terminals.
3. Touch the bare ends of the two wires to the metal ends of the fuse.
4. Observe the strip of metal again.

A Closer Look

The fuse overheated, or blew, when you added the electrical current. Fuses are electrical devices that stop the flow of electricity automatically when they overheat. The metal strip that carries the current in the fuse is designed to melt (or blow) at a certain temperature. When it blows, it stops the flow of electricity.

Attention!

Use caution when handling the glass fuse. It may get hot when hooked up to the battery.

35

Funny Fountain

15 minutes

What You Will Do

Demonstrate the reaction of hot and cold gases.

Get it Together

- Small jar with screw-on lid
- Hammer and thick nail
- Plastic straw
- Long candle
- Match
- Hot tap water
- Large, empty coffee can
- Ice cubes
- Scissors

Procedure

1. Use the hammer and nail to make a hole in the center of the lid of the small jar. The hole should be large enough to fit the straw through it.
2. Cut the straw in half and push one piece halfway through the hole in the lid.
3. Light the candle and let it burn until the wax on top begins to melt. Drip some hot wax around the edge of the hole so it seals the straw in the lid.
4. Fill the coffee can ³/₄ full with water and ice cubes.
5. Fill the jar with hot water and empty it several times to thoroughly heat the jar.
6. Quickly screw the lid on the jar.
7. Place the jar, lid-side down, into the can of ice water.
8. Look underneath to see the water shoot out.

A Closer Look

A fountain of water shoots out of the straw. Hot air needs more space than the same amount of cold air. When you put the jar into the cold water, the air in the jar cooled very quickly and began to contract, thus reducing the air pressure. The air pressure on the surface of the cold water was now higher than the air pressure inside the jar, and this pressure difference then pushed the cold water up the straw and into the jar.

Attention!

Use caution when working with the hammer, matches, and scissors.

36

Heat Energy

Hot, Hot Chocolate

5 minutes

What You Will Do

Show evidence of the sun's heating ability.

Get it Together

◆ Chocolate bar
◆ Magnifying glass
◆ Bowl or plate
◆ Sunny day

A Closer Look

Our sun has an intense output of heat and light energy. The magnifying glass focuses the rays of the sun into a small, compact area, causing the chocolate to heat up much faster.

Procedure

1. Unwrap the chocolate bar and place it on the plate.
2. Go to a sunny window or go outdoors, and use the magnifying glass to focus the sunlight on the chocolate.

What Now?

Use different types of magnifying glasses and different types of chocolate bars. Time how long each takes to melt.

Rusty Wool

5 minutes

What You Will Do

Demonstrate how a chemical reaction can produce heat.

Get it Together

- 1 steel wool pad without soap
- ¼ cup of vinegar
- Cooking or outdoor thermometer
- Jar with lid (thermometer must fit inside the closed jar)
- Bowl

Procedure

1. Place the thermometer inside the jar and close the lid. Record the temperature after five minutes and remove the thermometer.
2. Soak the steel wool in a bowl of vinegar for three minutes.
3. Squeeze out any extra liquid from the steel wool and wrap it around the bulb of the thermometer.
4. Place the thermometer and the steel wool inside the jar and close the lid.
5. Record the temperature after five minutes.

A Closer Look

The vinegar removes any protective coating from the steel wool, allowing iron in the steel to form iron oxide, commonly known as rust. Rusting is a slow chemical reaction between iron and oxygen, in which heat energy is released. The heat released causes the temperature to rise.

Clean Up

Put the steel wool in the trash.

Sweet as Sugar

5 minutes

What You Will Do

Demonstrate a catalyst at work.

Get it Together

◆ Sugar cube
◆ Tin pan
◆ Fireplace or charcoal ash
◆ Match

Procedure

1. Place a piece of sugar cube in a tin pan and try to set it on fire.
2. Dab a corner of the cube with ash and try to set it on fire again.

A Closer Look

The sugar begins to burn with a blue flame until it is completely gone. The sugar cannot be lighted separately, but the ash can initiate the combustion. A substance which brings about a chemical reaction, without itself being changed, is called a catalyst.

Attention!

Do only under adult supervision. Use caution when working with matches.

39

Heat Energy
Three Candle Race

5 minutes

What You Will Do

Demonstrate that fire needs oxygen to burn.

Get it Together

◆ 3 identical candles and holders
◆ Medium-sized empty glass
◆ Large-sized empty glass
◆ Matches

Procedure

1. Light the candles.
2. Place the glasses over two of the candles.
3. Observe which candle is the first to extinguish.

A Closer Look

Flames require oxygen in the air in order to burn. The candle with an unlimited air supply will burn for a long time. The candle in the large glass has more air, so it will burn longer than the candle in the small glass.

Attention!

Do only under adult supervision. Use caution when working with matches.

Why is Popcorn Popcorn?

15 minutes+

What You Will Do

Demonstrate that moisture inside popcorn kernels and heat are key factors in popping corn.

Get it Together

- Hot air popcorn popper
- ¼ cup fresh popcorn
- ¼ cup dried popcorn (to dry kernels, place a single layer on a tray in an oven at 190° F for about eight hours)
- Measuring cup

Procedure

1. Pop the fresh popcorn.
2. Pop the dried popcorn.
3. Measure the volume of each. Compare.

A Closer Look

Fresh popcorn should produce a higher volume of popped corn. Popcorn is mostly starch and water. As the corn is heated, the water inside the kernel turns to steam. The pressure pushes against the outer layer of the kernel. This layer holds in the steam until the pressure builds up high enough to break the outer layer and the kernel explodes. The starch expands into a white jelly-like bubble. The dried kernels had most of the moisture evaporated from them, resulting in a smaller explosion and a smaller popped corn.

Attention!

Use caution when using the popcorn popper.

POPSTER

FRESH

DRIED

What Now?

Try different brands of popcorn to see which brand gives the highest volume of product.

41

Model Building
Gumdrop Molecules

10 minutes

What You Will Do

Model chemical structures of common molecules.

Get it Together

◆ Package of colorful gumdrops
◆ Toothpicks

Procedure

1. Separate the gumdrops by color.
2. Designate a different color to represent chemical elements: carbon, hydrogen, and oxygen.
3. Make a model of a water molecule by connecting two of the same color gumdrops (hydrogen) to one different color gum drop (oxygen) with toothpicks.
4. Connect one carbon to two oxygens (CO_2) using two toothpicks for each link.
5. Connect 2 oxygens together with two toothpicks (O_2).
6. What other molecular combinations can you model?

A Closer Look

Since scientists cannot see molecules they use models. Compounds contain two or more atoms connected together with a chemical "glue" called a bond. Your toothpick represents the chemical bond. Some compounds are held together by single bonds, others are held together with double bonds.

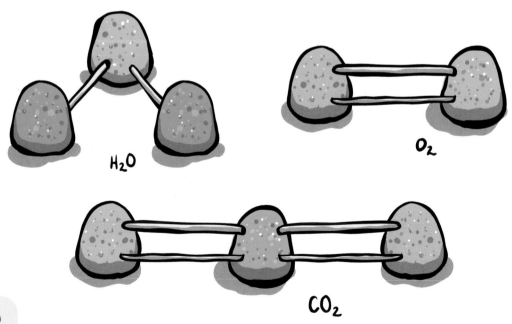

H_2O

O_2

CO_2

Clean Up

Eat and enjoy.

42

Physical Change

Are You Mr. Write?

What You Will Do

Observe how carbon can reduce friction.

Get it Together

♦ Sharpened lead (graphite) pencil
♦ Two 1" square pieces of white paper

Procedure

1. Rub the two pieces of paper back and forth between your fingers.
2. Now rub pencil lead (graphite) on one side of each piece of paper. Try to get as much graphite as you can on the papers.
3. Rub the two pieces of paper together again with the graphite covered sides touching.

A Closer Look

The papers slide more easily when covered in graphite. Graphite is a form of carbon, one of the chemical elements found in all living things. Graphite is used in machines to lubricate or reduce friction between surfaces.

Attention!
Wash your hands when completed.

What Now?

Try using an ink pen or crayons to see if they reduce friction.

43

Physical Change
Bubbling Colors

1 minute

What You Will Do

Examine the sublimation of dry ice.

Get it Together

◆ Food coloring (several colors)
◆ Several tall jars
◆ Several chunks of dry ice
◆ Water

Procedure

1. Fill the jars with water.
2. Place a few drops of food coloring in each jar. Stir.
3. Add a chunk of dry ice to each jar.

A Closer Look

The water's temperature is higher than that of the dry ice, and this causes the dry ice to sublime, or turn from a solid into a gas, faster than normal. The carbon dioxide bubbles escape with such a force that it resembles boiling water. The food coloring is just for effect.

Attention!
Use caution when working with dry ice. Wear gloves because it can burn your skin. Do only under adult supervision.

Clean Up

Allow the ice to completely evaporate, then pour the water down the drain.

Expando

10 minutes

What You Will Do

Demonstrate how pressure affects the volume of a marshmallow.

Get it Together

- Fresh marshmallow
- Small, clear, glass bottle with a mouth slightly larger than the marshmallow
- Black marker
- Modeling clay
- Drinking straw

Procedure

1. Use the marker to draw a face on the marshmallow.
2. Place the marshmallow inside the glass bottle.
3. Wrap the clay around the straw about 1" from its end.
4. Completely seal the short end of the straw in the bottle.
5. Suck (inhale) the air out of the bottle and observe the marshmallow.
6. Release the straw from your mouth and observe.

A Closer Look

A marshmallow is a spongy solid that contains sugar and air. Drawing the air out of the bottle decreases the pressure inside the bottle causing the air bubbles inside the marshmallow to expand. Removing the straw from your mouth allows the air pressure to return to normal, causing the marshmallow to return to its original size.

What Now?

You can stand in front of a mirror to see the results of your own marshmallow.

Physical Change
Food Detective

What You Will Do

Demonstrate that certain foods contain fat.

Get it Together

- Notebook paper
- Pencil
- Light source (the sun works fine)
- Several of your favorite foods

Procedure

1. Equally divide the notebook paper into as many sections as needed, depending on the number of food products to be tested.
2. Label each section with the food name.
3. Gently press the food product into the correct space.
4. Leave the foods on the paper for five minutes.
5. Remove the foods and throw them in the trash.
6. Allow the paper to dry for 10 minutes.
7. Hold the paper up to the light.
8. Determine if a translucent spot appears. This means the presence of fat.

A Closer Look

If some spots on your paper disappear, it means those products are mostly water. If oily-looking spots remain, it means those products contain fat. Fat and water lodge between the fibers of your paper and, while water can evaporate, the fat molecules remain trapped in the paper where they transmit light.

Homemade Ice Cream

30 minutes

What You Will Do

Demonstrate how ice cream is made through a physical change.

Get it Together

- 1 lb. coffee can with lid
- 3 lb. coffee can with lid
- Several rubber-bands
- 2-3 lbs. crushed ice
- 1½ cups whipping cream
- ¼ cup sugar
- 2 tsp. vanilla
- Mixing bowl and spoon
- Measuring spoons or cups
- Plastic wrap
- Box of salt

A Closer Look

Salt lowers the freezing point of ice. This chilly combination absorbs heat from the mixture inside the small can, allowing it to get colder faster. Slow freezing would cause large crystals to form, but this fast freezing keeps the mixture creamy.

Procedure

1. Place the whipping cream, sugar, and vanilla in the small can.
2. Place the lid on the can.
3. Cover the small can with plastic wrap and secure with the rubber bands.
4. Place a 2" layer of crushed ice in the bottom of the large can.
5. Sprinkle some of the salt over the ice.
6. Place the small can in the center of the large can.
7. Continue to fill the large can with crushed ice. Layer crushed ice and salt until the can is almost full.
8. Place the lid on the large can.
9. Sit on the floor and roll the can back and forth. Check every 10 minutes to see if your homemade ice cream is frozen.

Attention!
Do not eat the salt and ice mixture.

Clean Up

Eat the ice cream. Flush the ice and salt water down the sink.

47

Physical Change
I've Got a Good Solution

2 minutes

What You Will Do

Observe solubility of salt and pepper.

Get it Together

- ◆ 2 clear glasses
- ◆ 1 tsp. salt
- ◆ 1 tsp. pepper
- ◆ Water

Procedure

1. Fill each glass about half full with water.
2. Place the pepper in the first glass and stir.
3. Place the salt in the second glass and stir.

A Closer Look

The pepper is only floating in the water, an example of what is called a suspension. The salt, on the other hand, gets completely surrounded by charged water molecules, dissolving them into a uniform salt-water solution. Salt is said to be much more soluble than pepper.

Physical Change
Magic Balloon

What You Will Do

Observe the process of sublimation.

Get it Together

- Good quality large balloon
- Dry ice

Procedure

1. Place a quarter-size piece of dry ice inside a balloon.
2. Tie the neck tightly.

A Closer Look

The balloon will slowly inflate. At room temperature solid dry ice, which is solid carbon dioxide, changes directly into a gas without ever becoming a liquid. This process is called sublimation. When the solid carbon dioxide sublimes, the gas requires a much larger space, and since it cannot escape through the neck, it blows up the balloon instead.

Attention!

Use gloves when working with dry ice. It can cause severe burns. Do only under adult supervision. If the balloon is too small or the dry ice is too large, the balloon will burst.

49

Physical Change

Mayonnaise Maniac

15 minutes

What You Will Do

Make an emulsion.

Get it Together

- ◆ 1 cup salad oil
- ◆ 2 Tbsp. vinegar
- ◆ 2 eggs

- ◆ Clear jar with lid
- ◆ Measuring cups and spoons
- ◆ Salt and pepper

A Closer Look

You made mayonnaise. Mayonnaise is an emulsion, or a liquid in another liquid. The egg is the emulsifier, or "glue," that allows the oil to mix with the vinegar.

Procedure

1. Crack the eggs and place them in the jar.
2. Add 3 tablespoons of oil to the jar. Cap it and shake 15 times.
3. Pour half the oil, a little at a time, into the jar and shake 15-20 times between each addition.
4. Add the vinegar and shake.
5. Repeat Step 3 with the remainder of the oil.
6. Season to taste with salt and pepper. Refrigerate.

Clean Up

Enjoy your homemade mayo on your favorite foods.

1+1 Does Not Equal 2

5 minutes

What You Will Do

Show that water displaces air.

Get it Together

◆ Clear, glass quart jar
◆ White granular sugar
◆ Liquid measuring cup
◆ Masking tape
◆ Pen

Procedure

First you need to make your measuring jar:
1. Place a strip of masking tape vertically down the outside of the jar.
2. Pour exactly one cup of water into the jar.
3. Mark the water level on the tape with the pen.
4. Add a second cup of water to the jar and mark the water level on the tape.
5. Empty and dry the measuring jar.

Now for the experiment:
1. Pour exactly 1 cup of sugar in your measuring jar. Make sure the top of the sugar is at the 1 cup mark.
2. Add 1 cup of water.
3. Stir and observe the water level.

A Closer Look

The liquid level is actually below the two-cup mark on the tape. This is because a dry cup of sugar contains a lot of air. Air actually sits between all of the individual sugar particles. When sugar is dissolved in water, the water completely surrounds each sugar molecule, squeezing out the air. The displaced air leaves the solution and joins the atmosphere, resulting in a volume that is slightly less than the two cups.

What Now?

Try other solids in place of sugar.

Physical Change
Reusable Tissues

5 minutes

What You Will Do

Demonstrate the properties of waterproofing repellant.

Get it Together

- ◆ Shoe or boot waterproofing repellant
- ◆ Facial tissue
- ◆ 2 clear, plastic cups
- ◆ 2 rubber bands
- ◆ Water

Procedure

1. Open one tissue and drape it over one cup.
2. Push the center of the tissue slightly into the cup, forming a pocket. Secure the tissue with a rubber band.
3. Half fill the other cup with water, and pour some of that water into the pocket. Observe.
4. Repeat Step 1, but this time spray waterproofing repellant on the tissue.
5. Repeat Steps 2 and 3. Observe.

What Now?

Try the same test on different materials.

Physical Change

Secret Messages

5 minutes+

What You Will Do

Demonstrate the use of invisible ink.

Get it Together

- Cotton swab or toothpick
- Lemon juice
- Table salt
- Pencil or crayon
- Small cup
- Notebook paper

Procedure

1. Pour a small amount of lemon juice in the cup.
2. Dip the cotton swab or toothpick in lemon juice.
3. Write your secret message on the paper. Do not soak the paper with the juice.
4. Sprinkle salt on the entire message and allow it to dry (30 minutes.)
5. Brush away the salt crystals. Place the salt in the trash.
6. Gently rub a sharp pencil (at an angle) or crayon back and forth across the paper several times until the message appears.

A Closer Look

When you brush away the salt you leave a trail of small salt crystals with sharp edges on your message. As you rub the pencil over the paper, you are adding more carbon to the salt crystals than to the rest of the paper. The lemon juice acts as a "glue" for the salt.

Shake, Shake, Shake!

5 minutes

What You Will Do

Illustrate how some substances are soluble in water.

Get it Together

- ◆ 4 covered jars
- ◆ Warm tap water
- ◆ 3 Tbsp. each of sand, sugar, salt, and oil

Procedure

1. Place warm water in each of the four jars.
2. Place one of each substance, sand, sugar, salt, and oil, in each of the four jars.
3. Cap all the jars and shake them for one minute.

A Closer Look

Sugar and salt are soluble solids in water and will dissolve. Oil is hydrophobic (water-hating) and forms insoluble drops, while the insoluble sand simply settles at the bottom.

Attention!

Use caution when working with warm water.

Clean Up

Flush all liquids down the drain with water. Allow the sand to settle to the bottom, spill off the water and discard the sand in the trash.

What Now?

Try different household substances to see if they dissolve in water.

54

Soap Soup

What You Will Do

Illustrate how soapy water can form soap.

Get it Together

- 5 Tbsp. laundry flakes
- Hot water
- 4 Tbsp. salt
- 2 large cups
- Tablespoon
- Measuring cup

A Closer Look

Salt causes the liquid soap to separate into two layers. The solid layer called neat soap rose to the top.

Attention!

Use caution when working with hot water.

Procedure

1. Place a cup of hot water in one cup.
2. Add the laundry flakes and stir until dissolved.
3. Place another cup of hot water in the second cup and dissolve the salt in the water by stirring.
4. Slowly, pour the salt water on top of the soapy water.
5. Wait a few minutes.

What Now?

Add a little perfume and coloring to the soap.

55

Sweets for my Sweet

15 minutes+

What You Will Do

Demonstrate how temperature changes the form of a substance.

Get it Together

- 2 cups granulated sugar
- $\frac{1}{8}$ tsp. cream of tartar
- $\frac{2}{3}$ cup water
- Few drops of food coloring
- Small pot (about 1 quart)
- Cooking spoon
- Small bowl of cold water
- Heat source
- Flat cookie sheet
- Margarine

Procedure

1. Rub the cookie sheet with a thin layer of margarine.
2. Place the sugar, cream of tartar, water, and food coloring in the pot. Stir.
3. Heat the mixture until it boils. Boil for three minutes.
4. Test your candy by placing the spoon in the mixture and dripping it over the bowl of water. (Caution: It is very hot.) If the mixture turns hard in the water it is done. If it is still not hard, heat it for another minute and repeat this step.
5. Carefully pour the hot mixture onto the cookie sheet.
6. Allow to cool for one to two hours.
7. Break it up, eat, and enjoy.

A Closer Look

You made rock candy. In this demonstration, you changed the state of sugar from a solid to a liquid, and back to a solid again by changing the temperature. The cream of tartar acts as a thickener.

Attention!

As with any hot item, caution should be used.

The Escaping Smell Mystery
15 minutes

What You Will Do

Display how gas molecules can seep through a solid.

Get it Together

- ◆ 3 balloons
- ◆ Funnel
- ◆ A few drops of vanilla extract, soy sauce, and lemon juice

Procedure

1. Use the funnel to place a few drops of vanilla extract inside a balloon. Inflate the balloon and tie it.
2. Repeat Step 1 with the soy sauce and lemon juice.
3. After 10 minutes, smell the outside of each balloon.

A Closer Look

All things are made up of tiny particles called molecules. Since you could smell the vanilla, soy sauce, and lemon juice, their molecules are small enough to sneak through the larger rubber balloon molecules.

Physical Change
The Thirsty Potato

2 minutes+

What You Will Do

Show how salt extracts water from a potato.

Get it Together

- Fresh potato
- Salt
- Spoon

Procedure

1. With the spoon, scoop a hole in the side of the potato.
2. Place a spoonful of salt in the hole.
3. Let the potato sit overnight.
4. Observe what is in the hole.

A Closer Look

The hole is filled with water instead of salt. A potato has a good deal of water in it. The salt acts like a paper towel and draws the water out of the potato. Meanwhile, the salt dissolved into the water.

What Now?

Try different vegetables measuring the amount of water that is drawn from each specific vegetable.

Polymers

Amazing Balloon

2 minutes

What You Will Do

Demonstrate the flexibility of a polymer.

Get it Together

- 8"-10" round balloon (helium quality)
- 12" or longer straight needle, pin, sharpened, round uphol-stery needle, or thin wooden skewer
- Vegetable oil

Procedure

1. Blow up the balloon, letting out a little air, and tie it off.
2. Pour a few drops of oil on the tip of the needle.
3. Stick the needle through the end of the balloon with a gentle, but quick motion. Make sure you place the needle close to where the tie is.
4. Gently push the needle all the way through the balloon exiting where the balloon looks the darkest. Use the same gentle, but quick motion.

Note: You may have to try this a few times to get it right, but once you do, you can amaze all your family and friends. Be patient.

A Closer Look

The balloon will not break, but will slowly deflate through the pin hole. The needle stretches the latex molecules apart without tearing the walls. Thus, the key to sticking the needle in is to pick the point where the latex is stretched the least. The oil prevents the popping by lubricating the needle so it can penetrate the elastic molecules.

Attention!

Do only under adult supervision. Use caution when working with sharp objects.

Bounce for the Ounce

2 minutes

What You Will Do

Demonstrate crosslinking in a polymer.

Get it Together

- ◆ A few ounces of liquid latex (party/balloon store)
- ◆ A few ounces of vinegar
- ◆ 2 small containers

Procedure

1. Pour the vinegar in one container, and the latex in the other.
2. Dip one finger up to the middle knuckle in the vinegar.
3. Immediately, dip that finger into the latex.
4. Allow the latex to dry on your finger for a minute.
5. Roll the latex off your finger as you would a stocking.

A Closer Look

The latex solidifies and forms a solid mass. Latex is made of small polymers (chains of molecules), and the vinegar randomly hooks these polymers together. The result is the solid rubber that formed around your finger.

Attention!

Latex is safe, however, keep it away from your face.

60

Play Clay

15 minutes

What You Will Do

Demonstrate how heat can change a mixture into a new substance.

Get it Together

- 1 cup flour
- 1 cup water
- ½ cup salt
- 1 tsp. cooking oil
- 2 tsp. cream of tartar

- Saucepan
- Heat source
- Spoon
- Food coloring (optional)

A Closer Look

Heat changed your mixture into a new substance. Heat initiates bond formation in many chemical reactions, including cooking. This toy clay is considered a polymer.

Procedure

1. Pour all the ingredients (except the food coloring) in the saucepan and mix them together with the spoon.
2. Cook the mixture slowly over medium heat. Add the food coloring at this time. Stir.
3. Keep stirring until the mixture looks like a big ball.
4. Remove from the saucepan and allow to cool.
5. Knead the Play Clay by pushing it back and forth with the palm of your hand.

Attention!

Use caution when working with a heat source. Do only under adult supervision.

Poly Want a "Mer"?

1 minute

What You Will Do

Provide a model for polymer formation using individual monomers.

Get it Together

◆ 2 Paper clips
◆ Paper bill

Procedure

1. Fold the bill in three sections, so it is s-shaped.
2. Clip the middle section to one of the end sections of the bill with a paper clip.
3. Clip the middle section with the remaining end of the bill with the other paper clip.
4. Grasp the two ends and quickly pull the bill back to its original shape.

A Closer Look

The paper clips linked together. Each paper clip represents a singular molecule, or monomer. The bill acts as a catalyst to aid in the joining of the two monomers. This reaction represents the chemical combination of monomers, which is called polymerization.

What Now?

Repeat the procedure using four or more clips to make larger polymers.

Pop Goes the Bottle

10 minutes

What You Will Do

Demonstrate the stretchability of polymers using hot air.

Get it Together

- Latex balloon
- Narrow-necked glass bottle (16 oz. pop bottle)
- Saucepan
- Stove or heat source
- Water
- Oven mitt

Procedure

1. Fill the pan about $\frac{1}{2}$ full of water and heat it. Allow the water to get at or near boiling.
2. Stretch the tip of the balloon over the neck of the bottle.
3. Place the bottle in the pan of hot water for a few minutes and observe.
4. Allow the bottle to cool. Observe.
5. Use an oven mitt or glove to remove the hot bottle from the stove upon completion of the experiment.

A Closer Look

Bond formation, or crosslinking, in latex occurs in a random, irregular fashion. This accounts for the stretchability of the balloon, allowing it to expand in the presence of the expanding hot air. If the monomers were crosslinked in an orderly, structured way, the balloon would be hard and rigid, and unable to stretch with the gas.

Attention!

This activity should be done under adult supervision. Do not stand too close to the balloon as it expands.

63

Super Duper Silly Glue

5 minutes

What You Will Do

Make a polymer.

Get it Together

- 2-3 ounces of white glue
- Borax powder
- Water
- 2 cups
- Liquid measuring cup
- Spoon
- Paper towels
- Food coloring (optional)

Procedure

1. Mix one cup of water with two tablespoons of borax powder in a cup.
2. Place a few ounces of glue in the second cup.
3. Put in the food coloring and stir.
4. Add two tablespoon of borax solution from Step 1.
5. Stir for a few minutes.
6. Over a trash can or paper towel, place the mixture in your hand and start to knead it for a few minutes.

A Closer Look

You have made a common children's toy that can be purchased at many toy stores. The glue is a polymer, a long chain of molecules, held together by a chemical crosslink, the borax. As the borax links more glue molecules together, the glue turns into a stiffened gel.

Attention!
The food coloring stains clothing.

Clean Up

Store your polymer in a sealable bag and it will last a long time.